Valuable stamps of Russia

THEODORE TSAVOUSSIS

ISBN:**1499729790**
ISBN-13:**978-1499729795**

DEDICATION

This book is dedicated to all stamp hobbyists, collectors,brokers, young and old.

CONTENTS

ACKNOWLEDGMENTS

Thank-you to all our readers.

Russia
1924 10k on 5r green type II, basic stamp wide "5", complete pane of 25, unique
Price : $800,000.00

Russia
1923 5r deep green, white paper, type II unissued wide "5", never hinged
Price $57,500.00

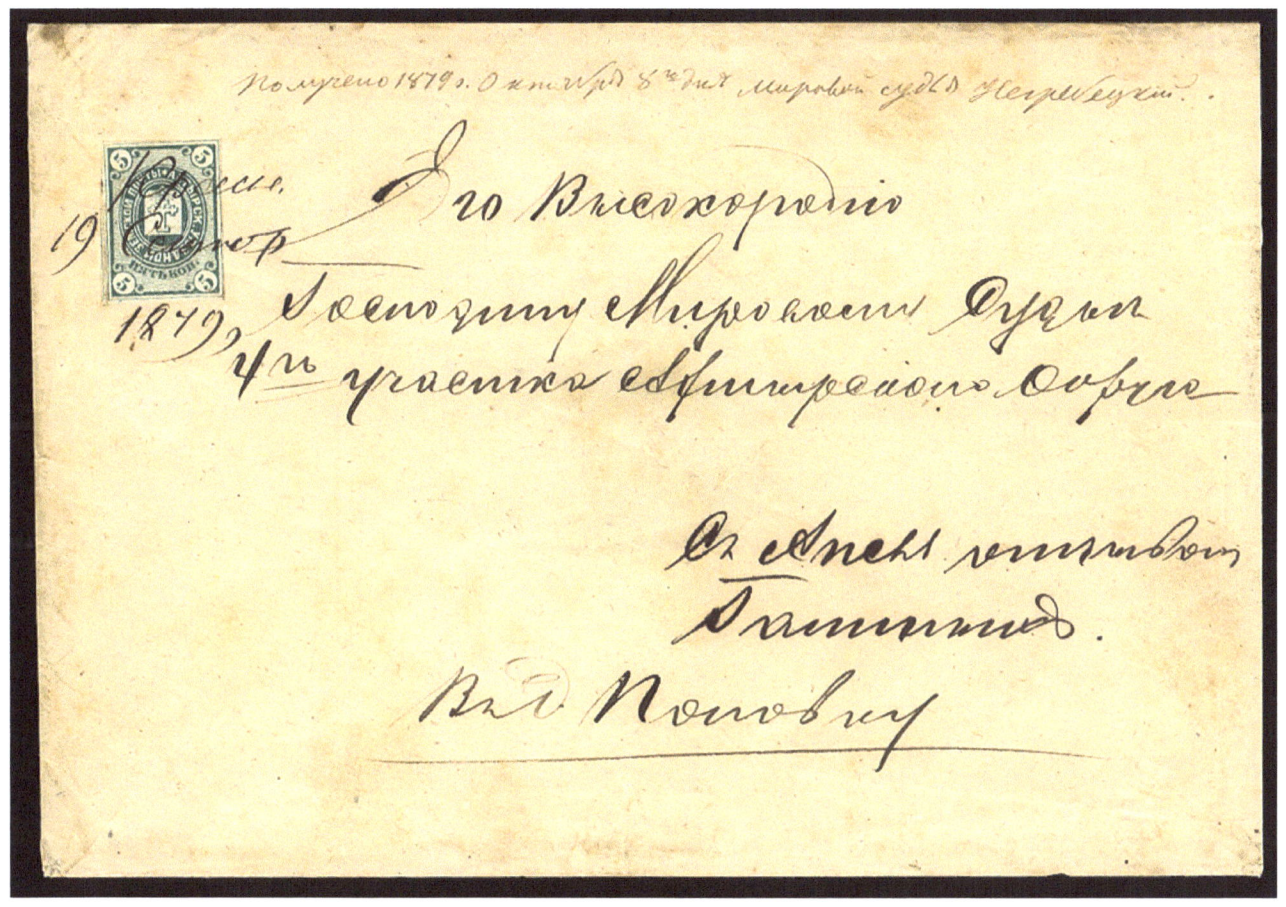

Russia - Zemstvo
AKHTYRKA 1879 (19 Sep) cover used locally within the district of Akhtyrka in the Kharkov
province franked with imperforate 5k green
Price : $71,875.00

Russia - Zemstvo
NOVAYA LADOGA 1883 (14 April) cover (petition) from Glazhevo village to Novaya Ladoga
town, franked with 5k blue and carmine,
Price $51,750.00

Russia
1935 Chelyuskin, 1k-50k blocks of four, complete set
Price : $74,750.00

Russia
1956 Definitives unissued 5k red (size 14,25x21,25mm), line-perf. 12 1/2 (instead of comb-
perf. 12x12 1/2 of the regularly issued stamp), the unique block of four
Price : $46,000.00

Russia
1902-5 5k red violet, vertically laid paper, groundwork inverted, lightly canceled
Price $77,625.00

Russia
1922-23 20r on 15k brown and violet blue, imperf. horizontal pair
Price : $32,200.00

Russia
1938 Trans-Polar Flight, 10k-50k imperforate horizontal pairs, set of four
Price : $27,600.00

Russia
1964 World Cruise, intended for "Khrushchev's Visit to Sweden"
Price : $28,750.00

Russia
1959 unissued 250th Anniversary of Battle of Poltava
Price: $25,300.00

Russia
1922 1k orange, major error overprint inverted and struck diagonally
Price : $24,150.00

1936 Pioneers, 15k blue, perf.14, unaccepted original design of Pioneer Salute
Price $12,650.00

Russia
1922 7,500r blue, horizontal watermark, gutter tete-beche block of four with sheet margin, never hinged and post office fresh
Price: $149,500.00

Russia
1959 40th Anniversary of the Soviet Circus, 60k red and blue, prepared but never issued (for political reasons
Price: $13,800.00

RUSSIA
All Soviet Philatelic Exhibition in Moscow, souvenir sheet of four on thick card, with the unique
three line personalized overprint "To the best shock worker of the All Russian Philatelic Society
- President of the Moscow Philatelic Organization E.M. Nurk
Price : $776,250.00

Russia
Rostov-on-Don Hunger Relief - Special Issue 1922 2,000r green (1), 6,000r (vertical pair) and 2,000r rose, vertical se-tenant, gutter/couche strip of four
Price : $195,500.00

Russia
1922 24 Germ "Marok" instead of "marki" on 3r, type IV, never hinged
Price : $138,000.00

Russian Consular Air Post
1922 1,200m on 50k, overprint type IV, lightly hinged, v.f., with Mikulski certificate. Type IV
occurs only twice per setting of 25, hence only four can exist
Price : $218,500.00

Russia
927 Esperanto, 14k imperf. block of four
Price : $24,150.00

Russia
Second Transpolar Flight, 20k selection of five different trial color proofs on ungummed stamp
paper, perf. 12, in violet, dark green, purple, black and red orange, each bearing "AHT-25"
(Antonov 25) inscription on wing (not on issued stamp)
Price : $115,000.00

Russia
1918 the legendary Nathan Altman imperforate sheetlet of 12 unissued designs
Price : $57,500.00

RUSSIA

1935 Anti War, set of five in blocks of four
Price $33,350.00

Russia
1930 Graf Zeppelin, set of two perforated and gummed proofs in issued colors, each
overprinted "IIPOEKT 8 September 1930" in red Cyrillic letters, probably unique
Price : $71,875.00

Russia
1934 Airships ("Pravda", "Lenin" etc.), complete set of five blocks of four, n.h. and post office
fresh
Price : $63,250.00

Russia

1932 International Polar Year, 50k carmine rose, perf. 10 1/2
Price : $29,900.00

Russia
1935 Moscow-San Francisco, small "f" used on registered and flown ppc (Sigismund
Levanevsky) from Moscow (C68b)
Price : $77,625.00

Russia
1856 10kop za lot, surface printed essay in blue, Mercury type, cut to shape and affixed on entire envelope
Price : $92,000.00

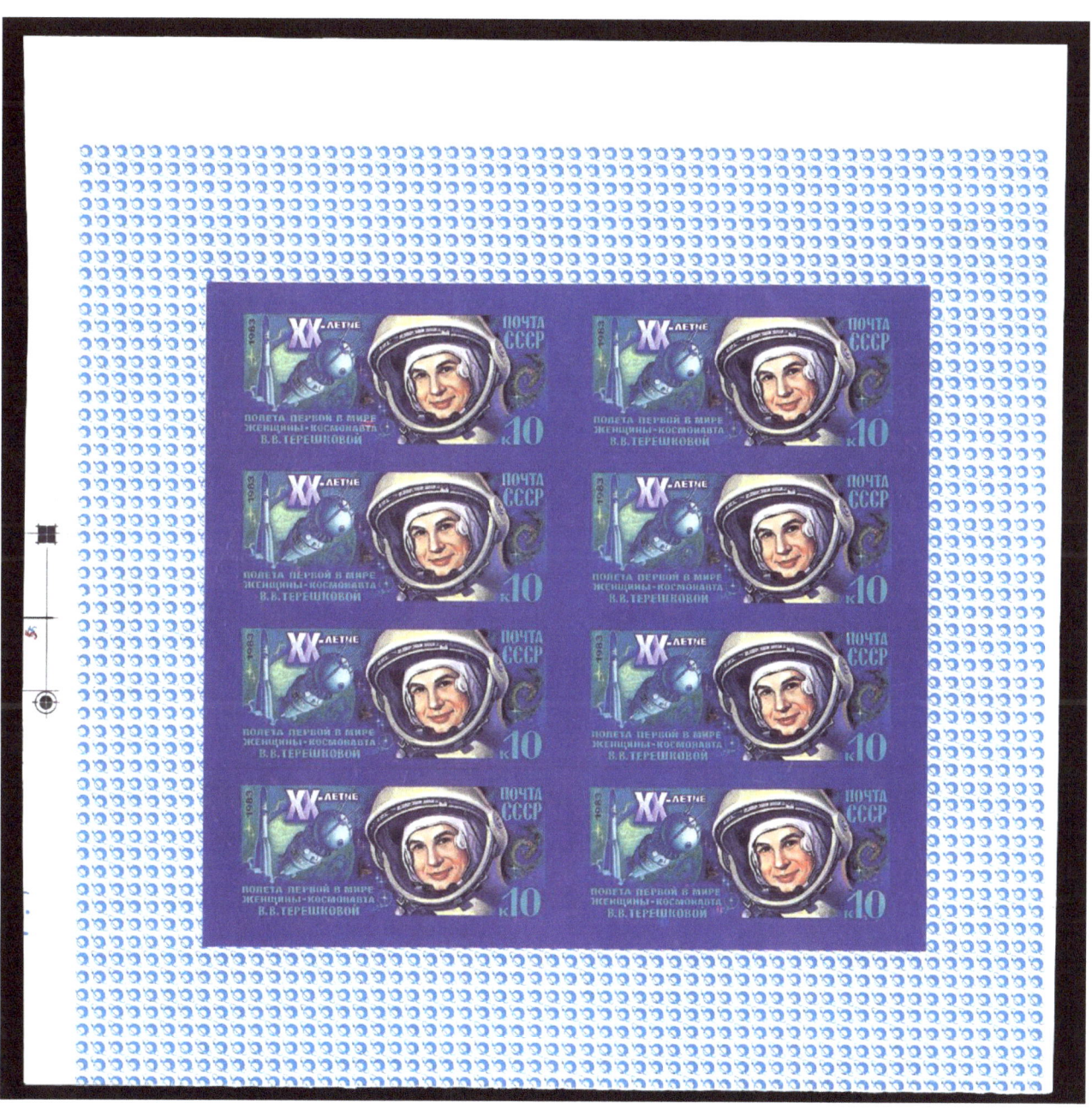

Russia
1983 Valentina Tereshkova, imperforate 10k sheetlet of eight, one of six known
Price : $83,375.00

Russian Air Post
1934 Stratosphere, 5k-20k, set of three imperforate sheet margins singles in issued colors
Price : $43,125.00

Russia
1856 "10kop za lot, 1k za konv:" (10k per 10 lot; 1kop for cover) embossed Eagle, in black, with greenish background, die essay on thin card
Price : $63,250.00

Russia
1935 Moscow-San Francisco, inverted overprint (C68a)
Price : $161,000.00

Russia
1935 Moscow-San Francisco, vertical block of six, positions 3-4, 8-9, 13-14, both of the middle stamps small "f",
Price : $195,500.00

Russian Telegraph Stamps
1866 20k black & brown, full original gum, less than 10 exist
Price: $46,000.00

Russia
1939 Steelworker, 15k dark blue, imperforate horizontal gutter pair
Price : $24,150.00

Russia
1858 10k brown and blue, thick paper, original gum (Scott 2)
Price : $14,950.00

:
Russia
1858 20k blue and orange, thin Paper, unused with original gum (Scott 3)
Price : $17,825.00

Russia
1858 30k carmine and green, thin paper, unused with full original gum, never hinged (Scott 4)
Price : $14,950.00

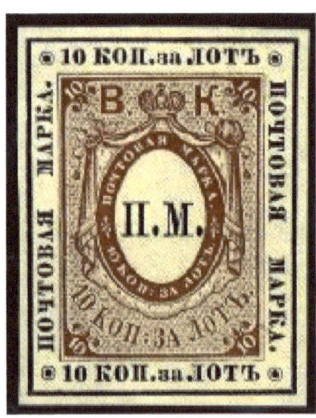

Russia
1864-65 10k brown & black, imperf. essay on gummed paper (some paper adheeions on back), center "II.M."
(Pochtowaya Marka), ex-Faberge
Price: $29,900.00

Russia
1884 3.50r black and gray, Horizontally Laid Paper, unused, small faults, one of five known
Price Realized: $57,500.00

Russia
1919 Hand with Sword Breaking Chains, money stamps, 1k orange, 2k green, perforated proof
sheetlets
Price : $71,875.00

Russia
1889 4k rose, horizontally laid paper, double impression, used, fine example of this
tremendous rarity, ex-Worthington
Price $13,225.00

Russia
1935 Spartacist Games, blocks of four
Price : $16,100.00

Russia
1879 7k gray and rose, watermarked horizontal hexagons, the famed "Perm" variety, one of
four known, ex-Ferrary (Mi.25z)
Price : $109,250.00

Russia
1858 20k blue & carmine rose, imperforate proof on thin unwatermarked paper
Price $19,550.00

Russia
1858 20k blue & orange, thick paper, unused with full original (#3)
Price : $10,925.00

Russia
1858 30k carmine & green, thin paper, unused with original gum, (#4)
Price : $12,075.00

Russia
1858 20k blue & orange, horizontal strip of three, with part of gutter at top, stamps n.h. (Mi.6, Scott 9)
Price: $18,400.00

Russia

1875 2k black & red, groundwork inverted, one of five known, ex-Ferrary, Mikulski cert.
Price : $46,000.00

Russia
1875 10k brown & blue, center inverted, only five are known, ex-Faberge, with Mikulski certificate (Mi.27xK)
Price: $66,125.00

Russia
1875 20k blue & orange, center double, unique copy
Price : $97,750.0

Russia
10k brown & blue, horizontal strip of three (1) Mikulski
Price : $17,250.00

Russia
10k brown and blue, sheet margin strip of three on cover (1) Mikulski
Price: $63,250.00

Russia
10k brown and blue, largest known franking (1) Mikulski
Price $33,200.00

Russia
Only known # 1 & 3 mixed franking on cover Mikulski
Price : $126,500.00

Russia
#2 horizontal strip of three, unique Mikulski
Price : $195,500.00

Russia
#4 Pair on cover Mikulski
Price $126,500.00

Russia

Largest Known Franking, #4 Mikulski
Price $264,500.00

Russia
1866 10k brown and blue, center inverted, two copied used on cover, unique, Mikulski cert.
€100,000+
Price : $132,000.00

ABOUT THE AUTHOR

Theodore Tsavoussis is an avid collector of stamps.